Your Temperament Can Be Changed

. . .

A Tyndale Treasure by
TIM LaHAYE

Tyndale House
Publishers, Inc.
Wheaton, Illinois

Your Temperament Can Be Changed! is
adapted from *Spirit-controlled Temperament*
by Tim LaHaye, copyright © 1966 by Post, Inc.,
LaMesa, California.

Library of Congress Catalog Card Number 72-84419
ISBN 0-8423-8750-1
Published by Tyndale House Publishers, Inc.
by arrangement with the copyright holder.
First printing, October 1978.
Printed in the United States of America.

CONTENTS

PREFACE

There is nothing more fascinating about man than his temperament! It is temperament that provides each human being with the distinguishing qualities that make him as different from his fellowmen as the differing designs God has given to snowflakes. It is the unseen force underlying human action, a force that can destroy a normal and productive human being unless it is disciplined and directed.

Temperament provides man with both strengths and weaknesses. Although we like to think only of our strengths, everyone has weaknesses!

God has given the Christian the Holy Spirit, who is able to improve man's natural strengths and overcome his weaknesses. The goal of this book is to help you understand how your temperament influences you, and how the Holy Spirit will help you overcome your weaknesses.

YOU'RE BORN WITH IT!

1 "Why can't I control myself? I know what's right and wrong—I just don't seem to be able to do it!" This frustrated plea was spoken by a young businessman who had come to me for counseling. It wasn't the first time I had heard that plaint in one form or another; in fact, it is a very common experience.

The Apostle Paul no doubt felt that same way when he said, " . . . for to will is present with me; but how to perform that which is good I find not. For the good that I would I do not: but the evil which I would not, that I do. Now if I do that I would not, it is no more I that do it, but sin that dwelleth in me" (Romans 7:18-20).

Paul differentiated between himself and that uncontrollable force within by saying, "It is no more I that do it, but sin that dwelleth in me." The "I" is Paul's person, the soul, will, and mind of man. The "sin" that dwelled in him was the natural weaknesses that he, like all human beings, inherited from his parents.

We have all inherited a basic temperament from our parents that contains both strengths and weaknesses. This temperament is called several things in

3

the Bible, "the natural man," "the flesh," "the old man," and "corruptible flesh," to name a few. It is the basic impulse of our being that seeks to satisfy our wants. To properly understand its control of our actions and reactions we should distinguish carefully between temperament, character, and personality by defining them.

Temperament

Temperament is the combination of inborn traits that subconsciously affects man's behavior. These traits are arranged genetically on the basis of nationality, race, sex and other hereditary factors. These traits are passed on by the genes. Some psychologists suggest that we get more genes from our grandparents than our parents. That could account for the greater resemblance of some children to their grandparents than to their parents. The alignment of temperament traits is just as unpredictable as the color of eyes, hair, or size of body.

Character

Character is the real you. The Bible refers to it as "the hidden man of the heart." It is the result of your natural temperament modified by childhood training, education, and basic attitudes, beliefs, principles, and motivations. It is sometimes referred to as "the soul" of man, which is made up of the mind, emotions, and will.

Personality

Personality is the outward expression of ourselves, which may or may not be the same as our character, depending on how genuine we are. Often personality is a pleasing facade for an unpleasant or weak character. Many are acting a part today on the basis of what they think a person should be, rather than what they really are. This is a formula for mental and spiritual chaos. It is caused by following the human formula for acceptable conduct. The Bible tells us, "Man looketh on the outward appearance, and God looketh on the heart," and "Out of the heart proceed the issues of life." The place to change behavior is inside man, not outside.

TEMPERAMENT CAN BE CHANGED!

2 The Apostle Paul put into words the heartcry of despair felt by every individual who laments his weaknesses of temperament: "Oh, wretched man that I am! Who shall deliver me from the body of this death!" (Romans 7:24) His answer is electrifying, "I thank God through Jesus Christ our Lord!"

Temperament can be changed! This is seen from II Corinthians 5:17: "Therefore if any man be in Christ, he is a new creature: old things are passed away; behold, all things are become new."

Since temperament is our "old nature," what man needs is a "new nature." That "new nature" is imparted to man when he receives Jesus Christ into his life. The Apostle Peter could speak on this subject from personal experience, for his temperament was vastly changed by receiving the "new nature." In II Peter 1:4 he refers to those who have been "born again" by faith in Jesus Christ as having become ". . . partakers of the divine nature, having escaped the corruption that is in the world through lust." The "divine nature" which comes through Jesus Christ is the only escape from the

6

control of our natural temperament, for only through Him are we made "new creatures."

There have been unusually self-controlled individuals who have changed part of their temperament and most of their conduct, but they have not cured all of their weaknesses. Even they have had their besetting sins. Satan, the "Prince of the power of the air," knows our major temperament weaknesses better than we do, and you can be sure he will use his power to defeat us. His greatest delight in regard to Christians is to see them defeated by their own weaknesses. The victory, however, is available through Jesus Christ whose Spirit can make all things new in the believer's life.

Admittedly, all Christians do not experience this transforming power. Just ask a convert's husband or wife, or in some cases, children! In fact, I'm sorry to have to admit that the majority of Christians do not see a *complete* transformation of their temperament. The reason is abundantly clear: the Christian has not remained in an "abiding" relationship with Jesus Christ. (See John 15:1-14.) But that does not change the fact that the moment the individual received Jesus Christ, he received the "new nature" which is able to cause "old things to pass away and all things to become new." We shall see that the filling of the Holy Spirit is not only commanded by God for every Christian (Ephesians 5:18), but this filling results in the Holy Spirit so controlling a man's nature that he actually lives the life of Christ. Before we come to that subject, however, we will examine the basic types of temperament so we know what to expect the Holy Spirit to do with us.

MEET THE FOUR
BASIC TEMPERAMENTS

3 More than 400 years before Christ, Hippocrates, the brilliant Greek physician and philosopher, propounded the theory that there are basically four types of temperament. He erroneously thought that these four temperament types were the result of the four body liquids that predominated in the human body: "blood"; "choler" or "yellow bile"; "melancholy" or "black bile"; and "phlegm." Hippocrates gave names to the temperaments that were suggested by the liquids he thought were the cause; the Sanguine —blood, Choleric—yellow bile, Melancholy— black bile, and Phlegmatic—phlegm. To him, these suggested the lively, active, black, and slow temperaments.

The idea that temperament is determined by body liquid has long been discarded, but strangely enough, the four-fold classification of temperaments is still widely used. Modern psychology has given many new suggestions for classification of temperaments, but none has found more acceptance than those of ancient Hippocrates. Perhaps the best known of the new classifications is the two-fold separation of "extrovert" and "introvert." These two do not provide sufficient separation for our purposes. We, therefore, shall present the four-fold temperament descriptions of Hippocrates.

The reader should bear in mind that the four-fold temperaments are basic temperaments. *No person is a single-temperament type.* We have four grandparents, all of whom make some contribution through genes to our temperament. They may all have been of different temperaments; therefore all men are a mixture of temperaments, although usually one predominates above the rest. There are varying degrees of temperament. For example, some may be 60 percent sanguine and 40 percent melancholy. Some are a blend of more than two, possibly all four, such as 50 percent sanguine, 30 percent choleric, 15 percent melancholy and 5 percent phlegmatic. It is impossible to determine ratios and blends, but that is not important. What is important for our purposes is to determine your basic temperament type. Then we can study your potential strengths and weaknesses, and offer a program for overcoming your weaknesses through the power of God in you.

There is a danger in presenting these four types of temperaments; some will be tempted to analyze their friends and think of them in the framework of, "What type if he?" This is a deceptive and precarious practice. Our study of temperaments should be for *self-analysis only,* except to make us more understanding of the natural weaknesses or short-comings of others. Now I would like you to meet . . .

The Sanguine

Sparky Sanguine is the warm, buoyant, lively and "enjoying" temperament. He is receptive by nature, and external impressions easily find their way to his heart, where they readily cause an outburst of response. Feelings predominate to form his decisions rather than reflective thoughts.

Mr. Sanguine has an unusual capacity to enjoy himself and usually shares his hearty nature. When he comes into a room of people, he has a tendency to lift the spirits of everyone present by his exuberant flow of conversation. He is a thrilling story teller because his warm, emotional nature almost makes him relive the experience in the very telling of it.

Mr. Sanguine never lacks for friends. Ole Hallesby said, "His naive, spontaneous, genial nature opens doors and hearts to him." He can genuinely feel the joys and sorrows of the person he meets and has the capacity to make him feel important, as though he were a very special friend, and he is—as is the next person he meets who then receives the same attention.

He enjoys people, does not like solitude, but is at his best surrounded by friends where he is the life of the party. He has an endless repertoire of interesting stories which he tells dramatically, making him a favorite with children as well as adults, and usually gaining him admission at the best parties or social gatherings.

Mr. Sanguine is never at a loss for words. He often speaks before thinking, but his open sincerity has a disarming effect on many of his listeners, causing them to respond to his mood. His free-wheeling, seemingly exciting, extroverted way of life often makes him the envy of the more timid temperament types.

His noisy, blustering, friendly ways make him appear more confident than he really is, but his energy and lovable disposition get him by the rough spots of life. People have a way of excusing his weaknesses by saying, "That's just the way Sparky is."

The world is enriched by these cheerful, sanguine people. They make good salesmen, hospital workers, teachers, conversationalists, actors, public speakers, and occasionally they are good leaders. The basic spiritual needs of the Sanguine temperament are the biblical "temperance (self-control), long-suffering, faith, peace and goodness."

Now meet the second temperament type:

The Choleric
Rocky Choleric is the hot, quick, active, practical, and strong-willed temperament. He is often self-sufficient, and very independent. He tends to be decisive and opinionated, finding it easy to make decisions for himself as well as for other people.

Mr. Choleric thrives on activity. In fact, to him, "life is activity." He does not need to be stimulated by his environment, but rather stimulates his environment with his endless ideas, plans and ambitions. His is not an aimless activity, for he has a practical, keen mind, capable of making sound, instant decisions or planning worthwhile, long-range projects. He does not vacillate under pressure of what others think. He takes a definite stand on issues and can often be found crusading against social injustice or unhealthy situations.

11

He is not frightened by adversities; in fact, they tend to encourage him. He has dogged determination and often succeeds where others fail, not because his plans are better than theirs, but because he is still "pushing ahead" after others have become discouraged and quit. If there is any truth in the adage, "Leaders are born, not made," then he is a born leader. Mr. Choleric's emotional nature is the least developed part of his temperament. He does not sympathize easily with others, nor does he naturally show or express compassion. He is often embarrassed or disgusted by the tears of others. He has little appreciation for the fine arts; his primary interest is in the utilitarian values of life.

He is quick to recognize opportunities and equally as quick at diagnosing the best way to make use of them. He has a well organized mind, though details usually bore him. He is not given to analysis, but rather to quick, almost intuitive appraisal; therefore, he tends to look at the goal for which he is working without seeing the potential pitfalls and obstacles in the path. Once he has started toward his goal he may run roughshod over individuals that stand in his way. He tends to be domineering and bossy and does not hesitate to use people to accomplish his ends. He is often considered an opportunist.

Mr. Choleric's attitude of self-sufficiency and strong will makes him spiritually calloused. If he becomes a Christian, this spirit makes it difficult for him to actively trust Christ for daily living. Choleric Christians porbably find it hardest to realize what Christ meant when he said, "Without me,

12

you can do nothing." There is no limit to what he can do when he learns to "walk in the Spirit" and to "abide in Christ." Of all the temperaments, he probably has the greatest number of spiritual needs, which are love, peace, gentleness, longsuffering, meekness and goodness.

Many of the world's great generals and leaders have been Cholerics. Mr. Choleric makes a good executive, idea man, producer, dictator, or criminal, depending upon his moral standards. Like Mr. Sanguine, he is usually an extrovert, although somewhat less in intensity.

Now I would like to have you meet the third temperament type . . .

The Melancholy

Maestro Melancholy is often referred to as the "black, or dark temperament." Actually he is the richest of all the temperaments, for he is an analytical, self-sacrificing, gifted, perfectionist type, with a very sensitive emotional nature. No one gets more enjoyment from the fine arts than the melancholy.

By nature he is prone to be an introvert, but since his feelings predominate he is given over to a variety of moods. Sometimes his moods will lift him to heights of ecstasy that cause him to act more extroverted. However, at other times he will be gloomy and depressed, and during these periods he is definitely withdrawn and can be quite antagonistic.

Mr. Melancholy is a very faithful friend, but unlike the Sanguine, he does not make friends easily. He will not push himself forward to meet

13

people, but rather lets people come to him. He is perhaps the most dependable of all the temperaments, for his perfectionist tendencies do not permit him to be a shirker or let others down when they are depending on him. His natural reticence to put himself forward is not an indication that he doesn't like people. Like the rest of us, he not only likes others but has a strong desire to be loved by them. Disappointing experiences make him reluctant to take people at their face value, thus he is prone to be suspicious when others seek him out or shower him with attention.

His exceptional analytical ability causes him to diagnose accurately the obstacles and dangers of any project he has a part in planning. This is in sharp contrast to the Choleric, who rarely anticipates problems or difficulties, but is confident he is able to cope with whatever problems arise. This characteristic often makes the Melancholy reticent to initiate some new project or opposed to those who wish to. Occasionally when he is in one of his great moods of emotional ecstasy or inspiration he may produce some great work of art or genius. These accomplishments are often followed by periods of great depression.

Mr. Melancholy usually finds his greatest meaning in life through personal sacrifice. He seems to have a desire to make himself suffer and will often choose a difficult life vocation involving great personal sacrifice. Once it is chosen, he is prone to be very thorough and persistent in his pursuit of it and is more than likely to accomplish great good.

No temperament has so much natural potential

14

when energized by the Holy Spirit as the Melancholy. But the temperament with the greatest strengths and potential is accompanied by what seems to be the largest of potential weaknesses. A Melancholy person may utilize his strengths to the point that he stands above his fellows, or he may be dominated by his weaknesses and become a neurotic, disconsolate, or hypochondriac-type individual who neither enjoys himself nor is enjoyed by others.

Many of the world's great genuises—artists, musicians, inventors, philosophers, educators, and theoreticians—were of the melancholy temperament. It is interesting to note that many outstanding Bible characters were either predominantly melancholy in temperament or had strong melancholy tendencies, such as Moses, Elijah, Solomon, the Apostle John and many others.

Now I would have you meet the fourth temperament type . . .

The Phlegmatic

Flip Phlegmatic gets his name from what Hippocrates thought was the body fluid that produced that "calm, cool, slow easy-going, well-balanced temperament." Life for him is a happy, unexcited, pleasant experience in which he avoids as much involvement as possible.

Mr. Phlegmatic is so calm and easy-going that he never seems to get ruffled, no matter what the circumstances. He has a very high boiling point and seldom explodes in anger or laughter, but keeps his emotions in control. He is the one temperament type that is consistent every time you see him. Beneath the cool, reticent, almost timid personality of Mr. Phlegmatic is a very capable combination of abilities. He feels much more emotion than appears on the surface and has a good capacity to appreciate the fine arts and the better things of life.

Mr. Phlegmatic does not lack for friends because he enjoys people and has a dry sense of humor. He is the type of individual that can have a crowd of people "in stitches" and never crack a smile. He has the unique capability of seeing something humorous in others and the things they do. He has a good, retentive mind and is often quite capable of being a good imitator. One of his great sources of delight is "needling" or poking fun at the other temperament types. He is annoyed by the aimless, restless enthusiasm of the Sanguine and often confronts him with his futility. He is disgusted by the gloomy moods of the Melancholy and is prone to ridicule him. He takes great delight in throwing ice water on the bubbling plans and ambitions of the Choleric.

He tends to be a spectator in life and tries not to get too involved with the activities of others. In fact, it is usually with great reluctance that he is ever motivated to any form of activity beyond his daily routine. This does not mean that he cannot appreciate the need for action and the difficulties of others. He and Mr. Choleric may see the same social injustice but their response will be entirely different. The crusading spirit of the Choleric will cause him to say, "Let's get a committee organized and do something about this!" Mr. Phlegmatic would be more likely to respond by saying, "These conditions are terrible! Why doesn't someone do something about this?" Mr. Phlegmatic is usually kindhearted and sympathetic but seldom conveys his true feelings. When once aroused to action, however, he proves to be a most capable and efficient person. He will not take leadership on his own, but when it is put on him he proves a capable leader. He has a conciliating effect on others and is a natural peacemaker. His primary needs are love, goodness, meekness, temperance and faith.

The world has greatly benefited by the gracious nature of the efficient Phlegmatic. He makes a good diplomat, accountant, teacher, leader, scientist, or other meticulous-type worker.

Now that you have met the four temperaments, you no doubt realize why "people are individuals." Not only are there four distinct types of temperaments that produce these differences, but the combinations, mixtures and degrees of temperament multiply the differences. In spite of that, however, most people reveal a pattern of behavior that indicates they lean toward one basic temperament.

Someone facetiously pointed out this sequence of events involving the four temperaments: "The hard-driving Choleric produces the inventions of the genius-prone Melancholy, which are sold by the personable Sanguine and enjoyed by the easygoing Phlegmatic."

The strengths of the four temperaments make each of them attractive, and we can be grateful that we all possess some of these strengths. But more

17

important, for our purposes, are their weaknesses. Our purpose is that you will diagnose your weaknesses and develop a program for overcoming them.

Dr. Hallesby summarized the weaknesses of the four temperaments in their relationships to other people in the following statement: "The Sanguine type enjoys people and then forgets them. The Melancholy is annoyed with people but lets them go their own crooked ways. The Choleric makes use of people for his own benefit; afterwards, he ignores them. The Phlegmatic studies people with supercilious indifference." This makes all the temperaments appear hopeless, but temperament is not character or personality or—more importantly—Spirit-controlled temperament.

o o o

THE SPIRIT-FILLED TEMPERAMENT

"The fruit of the Spirit is love, joy, peace, longsuffering, gentleness, goodness, faith, meekness, temperance..." Galatians 5:22-23.

4 The Holy Spirit-filled temperament does not have weaknesses; instead it has nine all-encompassing strengths. This is man as God intends him to be. It does not matter what one's natural temperament is; any man filled with the Holy Spirit, whether Sanguine, Choleric, Melancholy or Phlegmatic, is going to manifest these nine spiritual characteristics. He will have his own natural strengths, maintaining his individuality, but he will not be dominated by his weaknesses. The nine characteristics of the Spirit will transform his weaknesses.

All of these characteristics are found illustrated in the life of Jesus Christ. He is the supreme example of the Spirit-controlled man. A fascinating study of the life of Christ would be to catalog the illustrations of these nine characteristics as they appear in the Gospels. We shall mention some as we study each characteristic.

The first characteristic in God's catalog of Spirit-filled temperament traits is *love*. It is revealed as love both for God and for our fellowmen. The Lord Jesus said, "Thou shalt love the Lord thy God with all thy heart, and with all thy soul, and with all thy mind," and ". . . thou shalt love thy neighbor as thyself."

Very honestly, this kind of love is supernatural! A love for God that causes a man to be more interested in the Kingdom of God than in the material kingdom in which he lives is supernatural, for man by nature is a greedy creature. Love for his fellowman, which has always been a hallmark of the devout Christian, is not limited by temperament. True, Mr. Choleric as a Christian may need to go to the Holy Spirit for love more frequently than does Mr. Sanguine, but if the Spirit controls his life, he too will be a compassionate, tenderhearted, loving individual.

The second temperament characteristic of the Spirit-filled man is *joy*. R. C. H. Lenski, a great Lutheran theologian, gave this comment concerning the gracious emotion of joy. "Yes, joy is one of the cardinal Christian virtues; it deserves a place next to love. Pessimism is a grave fault. This is not fatuous joy such as the world accepts; it is the enduring joy that bubbles up from all the grace of God in our possession, from the blessedness that is ours, that is undimmed by tribulation. . . ."

No Christian can have joy if he depends upon the circumstances of life. The Spirit-filled life is characterized by a "looking unto Jesus, the Author and Finisher of our faith," which causes us to know that "all things work together for good to them that love God, to them that are the called according to his purpose" (Romans 8:28).

In the Scripture "joy" and "rejoicing" are frequently presented as expected forms of Christian behavior. They are not the result of self-effort but are the work of the Holy Spirit in your life, which causes you to "commit your way unto the Lord, and trust also in him." The Psalmist said in referring to the spiritual man's experience, "Thou hast put gladness in my heart more than they have when their grain and their new wine is increased" (Psalm 4:7).

This "fruit" of the Spirit is woefully lacking in many Christians today, which keeps them from being fruitful in the matter of winning people to Christ, because the world must see some evidence of what Jesus Christ can do in the life of the believer today in order to be attracted to Him. This supernatural joy is available for any Christian regardless of his basic or natural temperament. Jesus said, "These things have I spoken unto you, that my joy might remain in you, and that your joy might be full" (John 15:11). He also stated in John 10:10b, "I am come that they might have life, and that they might have it more abundantly." That abundant life will reveal itself in the Christian through joy, but it is only possible as he is filled with the Holy Spirit.

Martin Luther said, "God does not like doubt and dejection. He hates dreary doctrine, gloomy and melancholy thought. God likes cheerful hearts. He did not send His Son to fill us with sadness, but to gladden our hearts. Christ says: 'Rejoice, for your names are written in heaven.' "

The third temperament trait of the Spirit-filled

man is *peace*. Since the Bible should always be interpreted in the light of its context, it behooves us to examine the context. The verses just preceding this in Galatians 5 describe not only the works of the natural man without the Spirit, but also his emotions. His emotional turbulence is described by " . . . hatred, variance (strivings), jealousies, wrath, divisions and envyings." We readily see that the further man gets from God, the less he knows of peace.

The "peace" spoken of here is really two-fold. Someone has described it as "peace with God" and the "peace of God." The Lord Jesus said, "Peace I leave with you, my peace I give unto you . . ." (John 14:27). The peace He leaves us is likened to "peace with God." "My peace I give unto you" is likened to "the peace of God," for in the same verse He defines it as the peace of an untroubled heart: "Let not your heart be troubled, neither let it be afraid." The preceding verse, John 14:26, describes the coming of the Holy Spirit to believers as "the Comforter, which is the Holy Spirit." Thus we see that our Lord predicted the Holy Spirit would be the source of the "peace of God."

Peace *with* God, which is the "peace I leave with you," is the result of our salvation experience by faith. Man outside of Jesus Christ knows nothing of peace in relationship with God because his sin is ever before him and he knows he is accountable before God at the Judgment. This nagging fear robs man of peace with God all through his life. However, when this individual takes Jesus Christ at His word and invites Him into his life as Lord and

Savior, Jesus Christ not only comes in as He promised to do (Revelation 3:20), but He immediately cleanses all his sin (I John 1:7, 9). When the realization of God's forgiveness of his sin really grips his heart, man has peace with God. Romans 5:1 states it, "Therefore, being justified by faith, we have peace with God through our Lord Jesus Christ."

The peace *of* God, which is the antidote to worry, is not so automatically possessed by Christians as the peace *with* God. The "peace of God," which is untroubled in the face of difficult circumstances, is illustrated by the Lord Jesus who was sound asleep in the lower part of the ship while the twelve disciples were frightened beyond rationality. That ratio of twelve to one is very clearly evident among Christians today. It seems that when life's sea becomes turbulent through the raging winds of circumstance, twelve Christians will fret and fume and worry, while only one will have enough peace in his heart to trust God to take care of him in those circumstances. The twelve will be prone to worry all night, which further complicates their emotional, physical and spiritual life, while the one who "believes God" will get a good night's sleep, awaken refreshed and be available for God's use the next day. Circumstances should never produce our peace. We should look to God for peace; only He is consistent.

These first three characteristics, *love, joy* and *peace,* are emotions which very definitely counteract the most common weaknesses of temperament such as cruelty, anger, indifference, pessimism, gloom and criticism. They stand as adequate reasons for living the Spirit-filled life, but this is only the beginning.

The fourth temperament trait of the Spirit-filled man is *longsuffering*. Patience and endurance are the most prominent synonyms which have been suggested by Bible commentators for this spiritual characteristic. A very simple suggestion is, "Longsuffering means suffering long." It would be characterized by an ability to bear injuries or suffer reproof or affliction without answering in kind—as the Apostle Peter said about the Lord Jesus: " . . . who, when reviled, reviled not again." A longsuffering person is one who can do the menial, forgotten and difficult tasks of life without complaining or seething, but graciously, as unto the Lord. He finishes his task or suffers affronts while manifesting the loving Spirit of Christ.

The fifth characteristic of the Spirit-filled temperament is described in the King James Version as *gentleness*. Most of the modern translators of the Greek New Testament seem to change this to kindness or goodness, which make it almost synonymous with the next characteristic of the Spirit. In so doing, they tend to lessen the importance of this almost-forgotten form of behavior. It is a thoughtful, polite, gracious, considerate, understanding act of kindness which stems from a very tender heart. The world in which we live knows little of such tenderheartedness. It is the result of the compassion of the Holy Spirit for a lost and dying humanity.

The sixth characteristic of the Spirit-filled man

is called *goodness*, which is defined as "generous of self and possessions." It is benevolence in its purest sense. It includes hospitality and all acts of goodness that flow from the unselfish heart that is more interested in giving than receiving. Paul told Titus, the young preacher, that he should so preach that "they which have believed in God might be careful to maintain good works" (Titus 3:8). Man is so selfish by nature that he needs to be reminded by the Word of God and the indwelling Holy Spirit to occupy himself with goodness. It is obviously, then, a person who is more interested in doing for others than for himself.

All four of the natural temperaments are prone to be selfish and inconsiderate; thus all need this trait of goodness. It is particularly needed by those with Melancholy tendencies as a cure for depression and gloom, caused by an over-indulgence in self-centered thought patterns. There is something therapeutic about doing for others that lifts a man out of the rut of self-thought. As the Lord Jesus said, "It is better to give than to receive."

Many a Christian has cheated himself out of the blessing of the Holy Spirit's inspired impulse to do something good or kind for someone else by not obeying that urge. Instead of bringing joy to someone else's life by that act of kindness, the self-centered person stifles the impulse and sinks deeper and deeper in the slough of despondency and gloom. It is one thing to get good impulses; it is quite another to transmit them into acts of goodness. D. L. Moody once stated that it was his custom, after presenting himself to the Holy Spirit and asking to be led of the Spirit, to act upon those impulses which came to his mind, provided they did not violate any known truth of Scripture. Generally speaking, that is a very good rule to follow, for it pays rich dividends in mental health in the life of the giver.

The seventh trait of the Holy Spirit-filled man is *faith*. It involves a complete abandonment to God and an absolute dependence upon Him. It is a perfect antidote to fear, which causes worry, anxiety and pessimism.

In a vital way faith is the key to many other Christian graces. If we really believe God is able to supply all our needs, it is going to cause us to have peace and joy and will eliminate doubt, fear, striving and many other works of the flesh. Many of God's people, like the nation of Israel, waste forty years out in the desert of life because they do not believe God. Far too many Christians have "grasshopper vision." They are like the ten faithless spies who saw the giants in the land of Canaan and came home to cry, "We are as grasshoppers in their sight." How could they possibly know what the giants thought of them? You can be sure they did not get close enough to ask! They did just what we often do—jumped to a faithless conclusion.

The Bible teaches that there are two sources of faith. The first source is the Word of God in the life of the believer. Romans 10:17 states, "Faith cometh by hearing and hearing by the Word of God." The second is the Holy Spirit. Our text, Galatians 5:22-23, lists faith as a fruit of the Spirit. If you find that you have a temperament that is conducive to doubts, indecision and fear, then as a believer you can look to the filling of the Holy Spirit to give you a heart of faith which will dispel the emotions and actions of your natural nature, including fear, doubt, anxiety, etc. It will take time, however; habits are binding chains, but God gives us the victory in Christ Jesus. "Wait on the Lord; be of good courage, and he shall strengthen thine heart: wait, I say, on the Lord" (Psalm 27:14).

The eighth temperament trait of the Holy Spirit-filled man is *meekness*. The natural man is proud, haughty, arrogant, egotistical and self-centered, but when the Holy Spirit fills the life of an individual he will be humble, mild, submissive and easily entreated.

The greatest example in the world of meekness is the Lord Jesus Christ Himself. He was the Creator of the universe, and yet was willing to humble Himself, take on the form of a servant and become subject to the whims of humanity, even to the point of death, that He might purchase our redemption by His blood. Here we see the Creator of man buffeted, ridiculed, abused and spat upon by His own creation. Yet he left us an example of not reviling again.

This is particularly fortified when we recognize that all power and authority were given unto Him, even in the hours of His suffering. As He stated to Peter when He told him to put up his sword, "Thinkest thou that I cannot now pray to my Father, and he shall presently give me more than twelve legions of angels? But how then shall the Scriptures be fulfilled, that thus it must be?"

(Matthew 26:53-54) For our sakes He was meek that we might have everlasting life. He said of Himself, "I am meek and lowly in heart."

The final temperament trait characteristic of the Spirit-filled believer is *self-control.* The King James Version translates it "temperance," but really it is self-control or self-discipline. Someone has defined it as "self-controlled by the Holy Spirit."

Man's natural inclination is to follow the path of least resistance. Mr. Sanguine probably has more temptation along this line than any of the other temperament types, though who can say he himself has not given in to this very common temptation? "Self-control" will solve the Christian's problem of emotional outbursts such as rage, anger, fear, jealousy, etc., and cause him to avoid emotional excesses of any kind. The Spirit-controlled temperament will be one that is consistent, dependable and well ordered.

HOW TO BE FILLED
WITH THE HOLY SPIRIT

5 The most important thing in the life of any Christian is to be filled with the Holy Spirit! The Lord Jesus said, "Without me ye can do nothing." Christ is in believers in the person of His Holy Spirit. Therefore, if we are filled with His Spirit, He works fruitfully through us. If we are not filled with the Holy Spirit, we are unproductive.

It is almost impossible to exaggerate how dependent we are on the Holy Spirit. We are dependent on Him for convicting us of sin before and after our salvation, for giving us understanding of the Gospel, causing us to be born again, empowering us to witness, guiding us in our prayer life—in fact, for everything. It is no wonder that evil spirits have tried to counterfeit the work of the Holy Spirit and confuse His work. Satan places two obstacles before men: (1) he tries to keep them from receiving Christ as Savior, and (2) if he fails in this, he then tries to keep men from understanding the importance and work of the Holy Spirit.

God never makes it impossible for us to keep His commandments. So, obviously, if He commands us to be filled with the Holy Spirit, and He does, then it must be possible for us to be filled with His Spirit. I would like to give five simple steps for being filled with the Holy Spirit:

1. *Self-examination (Acts 20:28 and I Corinthians 11:28).* The Christian interested in the filling of the Holy Spirit must regularly "take heed" to "examine himself." He should examine himself, not to see if he measures up to the standards of other people or the traditions and requirements of his church, but to the previously described results of being filled with the Holy Spirit. If he does not find he is glorifying Jesus, if he does not have power to witness, or if he lacks a joyful, submissive spirit or the nine temperament traits of the Holy Spirit, then his self-examination will reveal those areas in which he is deficient and will uncover the sin that causes them.

2. *Confession of all known sin (I John 1:9).* "*If we confess our sins, he is faithful and just to forgive us our sins, and to cleanse us from all unrighteousness.*" The Bible does not put an evaluation on one sin or another, but seems to judge all sin alike. After examining ourselves in the light of the Word of God, we should confess all sin brought to mind by the Holy Spirit, including those characteristics of the Spirit-filled life that we lack. Until we start calling our lack of compassion, our lack of self-control, our lack of humility, our anger instead of gentleness, our bitterness instead of kindness, and our unbelief instead of faith, as sin, we will never have the filling of the Holy Spirit. However, the moment we recognize these deficiencies as sin and confess them to

30

God, He will "cleanse us from all unrighteousness."
Until we have done this we cannot have the filling
of the Holy Spirit, for He fills only clean vessels
(II Timothy 2:21).

3. *Submit yourself completely to God. (Romans 6:
11-13). "Likewise reckon ye also yourselves to be dead
indeed unto sin, but alive unto God through Jesus
Christ our Lord. Let not sin therefore reign in your
mortal body, that ye should obey it in the lusts thereof.
Neither yield ye your members as instruments of unrighteousness unto sin: but yield yourselves unto God, as
those that are alive from the dead, and your members
as instruments of righteousness unto God."* To be
filled with the Holy Spirit, one must make himself
completely available to God to do anything the
Holy Spirit directs him to do. If there is anything
in your life that you are unwilling to do or to be,
then you are resisting God, and this always limits
God's Spirit! Do not make the mistake of being
afraid to give yourself to God! Romans 8:32 tells us,
"He that spared not his own Son, but delivered him
up for us all, how shall he not with him also freely
give us all things?" It is clear from this verse that if
God loved us so much as to give His Son to die for
us, certainly He is interested in nothing but our
good; therefore, we can trust Him with our lives.
You will never find a miserable Christian in the
center of the will of God, for He will always accom-
pany His directions with an appetite and desire to
do His will.

Resisting the Lord through rebellion obviously
stifles the filling of the Spirit. Israel limited the Lord,

31

not only through unbelief, but, as Psalm 78:8 tells us, by becoming a "stubborn and rebellious generation; a generation that set not their heart aright and whose spirit was not steadfast with God." All resistance to the will of God will keep us from being filled with the Holy Spirit. To be filled with His Spirit, we must yield ourselves to His Spirit just as a man yields himself to wine for its filling.

Ephesians 5:18 says, "Be not drunk with wine . . . but be filled with the Spirit." When a man is drunk, he is dominated by alcohol; he lives and acts, and is dominated by its influence. So with the filling of the Holy Spirit, man's actions must be dominated by and dictated by the Holy Spirit. For consecrated Christians this is often the most difficult thing to do, for we can always find some worthy purpose for our lives, not realizing that we are often filled with ourselves rather than with the Holy Spirit, as we seek to serve the Lord.

When you give your life to God, do not attach any strings or conditions to it. He is such a God of love that you can safely give yourself without reservation, knowing that His plan and use of your life is far better than yours. And, remember, the attitude of yieldedness is absolutely necessary for the filling of God's Spirit. Your will is the will of the flesh, and the Bible says that "the flesh profiteth nothing."

Yieldedness is sometimes difficult to determine if we have already settled the five big questions of life: (1) Where shall I attend college? (2) What vocation shall I pursue? (3) Whom shall I marry? (4) Where shall I live? (5) Where shall I attend church? A Spirit-filled Christian will be sensitive to the Spirit's leading in small decisions as well as the big ones. But it has been my observation that many Christians who have made the right decisions on life's five big questions are still not filled with the Spirit.

4. *Ask to be filled with the Holy Spirit.* (Luke 11:13). *"If ye, then, being evil, know how to give good gifts unto your children: how much more shall your heavenly Father give the Holy Spirit to them that ask him?"* When a Christian has examined himself, confessed all known sin and yielded himself without reservation to God, he is then ready to do the one thing he must do to receive the Spirit of God. Very simply, it is to ask to be filled with the Spirit.

The Lord Jesus compares this to our treatment of our earthly children. Certainly a good father would not make his children beg for something he commanded them to have. How much less does God make us beg to be filled with the Holy Spirit which He has commanded. It is just as simple as that! But don't forget Step 5.

5. *Believe you are filled with the Holy Spirit! And thank Him for His filling.* "And he that doubteth is damned if he eat, because he eateth not of faith: for whatsoever is not of faith is sin" (Romans 14:23). "In everything give thanks: for this is the will of God in Christ Jesus concerning you" (I Thessalonians 5:18). For many Christians the battle is won or lost right here. After examining themselves, confessing all known sin, yielding themselves to God and asking for His filling, they are faced with a decision: to believe they are filled; or to go away in unbelief, in

33

which case they have sinned, for "whatsoever is not of faith is sin."

The same Christian, who when doing personal work tells the new convert to "take God at His Word concerning salvation," finds it difficult to heed his own advice concerning the filling of the Holy Spirit. He will tell a new babe in Christ, who lacks assurance of salvation, that he can know that Christ is in his life because He promised to come in if He were invited, and "God always keeps His Word." Oh, that the same sincere personal worker would believe God when He says: "How much more shall your heavenly Father give the Holy Spirit to them that ask him?" If you have fulfilled the first four steps, then thank God for His filling by faith. Don't wait for feelings, don't wait for any physical signs, but fasten your faith to the Word of God that is independent of feeling. Feelings of assurance of the Spirit's filling often follow our taking God at His Word and believing He has filled us, but they neither cause the filling nor determine whether or not we are filled. Believing we are filled with the Spirit is taking God at His Word, and that is the privilege given every Christian (Matthew 24:35).

GRIEVING THE HOLY SPIRIT
THROUGH ANGER

"Let no corrupt communication proceed out of your mouth, but that which is good to the use of edifying, that it may minister grace unto the hearers.

"And grieve not the holy Spirit of God, whereby ye are sealed unto the day of redemption.

"Let all bitterness, and wrath, and anger, and clamor, and evil speaking, be put away from you, with all malice:

"And be ye kind one to another, tenderhearted, forgiving one another, even as God for Christ's sake hath forgiven you." (Ephesians 4:29-32)

6 This text makes it very clear that we "grieve" the Holy Spirit of God through bitterness, wrath, anger, clamor, evil speaking and malice, which is enmity of heart. For some reason, otherwise consecrated Christians seem reluctant to face as sin these emotions that stem from anger. Galatians 5:20 lists hatred, strife and wrath in the same category as murders, drunkenness and revellings, saying, ". . . of the which I tell you before as I have also told you in time past, that they which do such things shall not inherit the Kingdom of God."

35

Anger—A Universal Sin

Anger is one of two universal sins of mankind. After counseling several hundred people, I have concluded that all emotional tension can be traced to one of two things: anger or fear. I cannot think of a single case involving individuals or couples who were upset but that the basic problem stemmed from an attitude that was angry, bitter and vitriolic, or fearful, anxious, worried and depressed. Dr. Raymond L. Cramer, another Christian psychologist, says in his book *The Psychology of Jesus and Mental Health:* "At times anxiety expresses itself in anger. A tense, anxious person is much more likely to become irritable and angry."[1] Anxiety is a form of fear; therefore, we can conclude that an angry person can also become a fearful person, and a fearful person can become an angry person. Anger grieves the Holy Spirit, and fear quenches the Holy Spirit, as we will point out in the next chapter.

In our study of the temperaments we found that the extrovertish sanguine and choleric temperaments are angry-prone, while the melancholy and phlegmatic are fear-prone. Since most people are a combination of temperaments, they could well have a natural predisposition to both fear and anger —if, for example, they are predominantly sanguine with possibly 30 percent melancholy tendencies. Then, too, from the statements cited from Dr. Brandt and Dr. Cramer, it would seem that the angry-prone temperament's expression of anger could cause fear, and the indulgence of the fear-prone habit of the melancholy and phlegmatic temperaments could cause the emotional problems of anger and hostility. It is my personal opinion that these two emotions bring more Christians into bondage to the law of sin than any other emotions or desires. Thank God there is a cure for these weaknesses through the Holy Spirit!

The High Cost of Anger
If man really understood the high price paid for pent-up wrath or bitterness and anger, he would seek some remedy for it. We shall consider the high cost of anger emotionally, socially, physically, financially, and most important of all, spiritually.

A. *Emotionally.* Suppressed anger and bitterness can make a person emotionally upset until he is "not himself." In this state he often makes decisions that are harmful, wasteful or embarrassing. We are intensely emotional creatures, designed so by God, but if we permit anger to dominate us, it will squelch the richer emotion of love. Many a man takes his office grudges and irritations home and unconsciously lets this anger curtail what could be a free-flowing expression of love for his wife and children. Instead of enjoying his family and being enjoyed by them, he allows his mind and emotions to mull over the vexations of the day. Life is too short and our moments at home too brief to pay such a price for anger.

Anger takes many forms. Many people do not regard themselves as angry individuals because they don't understand the many disguises anger takes. Consult the following chart for a description of the sixteen variations of anger.

BITTERNESS	WRATH
MALICE	HATRED
CLAMOR	SEDITIONS
ENVY	JEALOUSY
RESENTMENT	ATTACK
INTOLERANCE	GOSSIP
CRITICISM	SARCASM
REVENGE	UNFORGIVENESS

B. *Socially.* Very simply, an angry person is not pleasant to be around; consequently, those who are angry, grumpy or disgruntled are gradually weeded out of the social lists or excluded from the fun times of life. This is a price that a partner is often asked to pay for the anger of his mate, which in turn may increase their anger toward each other and limit what otherwise could be an enjoyable relationship.

C. *Physically.* It is difficult to separate the physical price paid for anger from the financial, because anger and bitterness produce so much stress which in turn causes physical disorder so that thousands of dollars are spent needlessly by Christian people for doctors and drugs. Doctors and medical associations today have released various statistics showing that from 60 to as high as 90 percent of man's bodily illness is emotionally induced, and anger and fear

38

are the main culprits! (Just think of the missionaries that could be sent to the foreign fields and the churches that could be built with 60 percent of the money Christians pay for medical expenses.)

If doctors are correct in their estimates, and we have no reason to believe they are not, this is money and talent wasted. How can our emotions actually cause physical illness? Very simply, for our entire physical body is intricately tied up with our nervous system. Whenever the nervous system becomes tense through anger or fear, it adversely affects one or more parts of the body.

Proverbs 4:23 says, "Keep thy heart with all diligence; for out of it are the issues of life." Therefore, the heart to which the writer of Proverbs referred was not the blood-pumping station we recognize as keeping our body in motion, but the emotional center located between our temples. In order for any body movement to take place, a message must be conveyed from the emotional center to the member to be moved.

If the emotional center is normal, then the functions of the body will be normal. If, however, the emotional center is "upset" or behaves in an abnormal manner, a reaction will be generated through the nervous system to almost every part of the body.

The three most important parts of man's being are: the will, the mind and the heart (or emotional center). Man is affected emotionally by what is placed in his mind. What he places in his mind is determined by his will; therefore, if man wills to disobey God and records things on the files of his

39

mind that cause emotions contrary to the will of God, these emotions trigger actions that displease God.

All sin begins in the mind! Man never commits sin spontaneously. Long before man commits murder he has harbored hatred, anger and bitterness in his mind. Before he commits adultery he has harbored lust in his mind.

His mind receives whatever his will chooses to read or hear, and his emotions will be affected by whatever he puts in his mind. That is why Jesus Christ gave the challenge to man, "Thou shalt love the Lord thy God with all thy heart, with all thy soul (will) and with all thy mind."

Many a doctor has been forced to tell heart patients, victims of high blood pressure, sufferers of colitis, goiter and many other common diseases: "We can find nothing organically wrong with you; your problem is emotionally induced." Usually the patient will become angry because he thinks the doctor means, "It's all in your mind." What the doctor means is, "It's all in your emotional center."

The increase in physical illnesses originating from our emotions has given rise to the use of tranquilizers and other emotion-depressants. These treatments are very limited in their lasting effect because they do not deal with the cause of the problem. Psychologists tell us that man is not able to fully control his emotions even by his will. I agree, for I have found that nothing short of the power of Jesus Christ is able to make an angry, bitter, vitriolic individual loving, compassionate, gentle and kind.

40

D. *Spiritually*. The highest price of all paid for an angry, bitter disposition is in the spiritual realm. Jesus Christ came to give us not only eternal life when we die, but abundant life here and now. That life can only be experienced by "abiding in Him" or "being filled with the Spirit." No man can abide in Christ or be filled with the Spirit who grieves the Holy Spirit, and "anger, bitterness, wrath, clamor and enmity of heart" grieve the Holy Spirit of God.

Grieving the Holy Spirit limits the work of God in an individual's life, keeps him from becoming mature in Christ Jesus, and hinders him from being the glowing, effective, fruitful Christian that he wants to be.

The Basic Cause of Anger

What causes a perfectly normal, likeable, congenial human being to suddenly react with heat and anger? The full realization and acceptance of the answer to that question provides the Christian with his first giant step toward its cure. Stripped of all the facade and fancy excuses for condoning anger, of calling it "old nick" or "my natural Irish disposition," we are confronted with an ugly word—*selfishness*. Although we love to excuse our weaknesses and justify them to ourselves as we nurse our grudges and indulge in angry, vengeful, bitter feelings, they are all motivated by selfishness. When I am angry, it is because someone has violated my rights and I am interested in myself. When I am bitter against someone, it is because they have done something against me, and again I come back to selfishness. Vengeance is always inspired by selfishness.

A lovely Christian lady came to my study to tell me her side of the problems in her home. When I confronted her with the fact of her angry, bitter spirit, she blurted out in her defense, "Well, you'd be angry too if you lived with a man who constantly ran roughshod over you and treated you like dirt!" Admittedly, he was not treating her the way a Christian man should, but her reaction could not possibly be caused by generosity; instead, it was plain old selfishness. The more she indulged in her selfishness and let anger predominate, the worse her husband treated her.

I confronted her with the fact that she had two problems. She looked at me rather startled and asked, "Did I hear you correctly—I have two problems? I only have one, my husband." "No," I said, "you have two problems. Your husband is one problem, but your attitude toward your husband is another. Until you as a Christian recognize your own sin of selfishness and look to God for a proper attitude, even in the face of these circumstances, you will continue to grieve the Holy Spirit of God." The change in that woman in almost one month's time was almost unbelievable. Instead of using her husband as an excuse to indulge in anger, she began to treasure her relationship to Jesus Christ more than the indulgence of her own selfishness. She went to Him who has promised to "supply all your needs according to His riches in glory by Christ Jesus" and began to experience victory over bitterness, wrath, anger, and all those emotional attitudes that grieved the Holy Spirit. Instead of waiting for a change in her husband's behavior, she literally changed her husband's behavior by hers. She told me that when God gave her victory over her own reaction to his miserable disposition, she began being kind to the one who was "despitefully using her," just as our Lord had instructed. Since love begets love and we reap what we sow, it was not long before the husband began to respond with kindness.

As fantastic as it may seem, I have observed this in the lives of those individuals who are willing to recognize inner anger and turmoil as the sin of selfishness and look to God for the grace, love, and self-control which He promises to them who ask Him. If you are reaping a crop of anger, bitterness and hatred, a little investigation will indicate to you that you have been *sowing* a crop of anger, bitterness and hatred. The Bible tells us, "Whatsoever a man soweth, that shall he also reap." If you had been sowing love, you would be reaping love. If you are not reaping love, may I suggest that you change the seeds you are sowing.

REFERENCES
1. Raymond L. Cramer, *The Psychology of Jesus and Mental Health*, © 1959, Cowman Publications, Inc., page 27, used by permission.

QUENCHING THE HOLY SPIRIT
THROUGH FEAR

"Rejoice evermore.

"Pray without ceasing.

"In everything give thanks: for this is the will of God in Christ Jesus concerning you.

"Quench not the Spirit." (I Thessalonians 5:16-19)

7 Quenching and grieving the Holy Spirit are the two sins one must guard against in order to maintain the Spirit-filled life. We have already seen that one grieves the Holy Spirit through anger. We shall now see that we quench the Holy Spirit through fear. Quenching the Holy Spirit is stifling or limiting Him. Neither grieving nor quenching the Holy Spirit eliminates Him from our life, but they do seriously restrict His control of our body which God would otherwise strengthen and use.

Our text indicates that the Spirit-filled Christian should be one who is able to "rejoice . . . always" (Philippians 4:4) and "in everything give thanks" (I Thessalonians 5:18). Anytime the Christian does not rejoice or give thanks in *everything*, he is out of the will of God. That does not mean only in good circumstances, for even the natural man rejoices in enjoyable circumstances. But when the

Scripture tells us "rejoice evermore" and "in everything give thanks," it means in any circumstance. Therefore, in order for man to give thanks for everything, he must live by faith. It is faith in God's love, God's power and God's plan for our lives that keeps us rejoicing through the Spirit in whatever circumstances we may find ourselves. An unhappy, unthankful attitude that quenches the Holy Spirit is caused by unbelief in the faithfulness of our God, which produces fear as we face the uncertain circumstances of life. Thus I would have you examine the subject of quenching the Holy Spirit through fear.

Fear Is Universal

The first reaction to the sin of disobedience on the part of Adam and Eve was one of fear. When Adam and Eve "heard the voice of the Lord God walking in the garden in the cool of the day . . . Adam and his wife hid themselves from the presence of the Lord God amongst the trees in the garden. And the Lord God called unto Adam and said unto him, where art thou? And he said, I heard Thy voice in the garden and I was afraid because I was naked and I hid myself" (Genesis 3:8-10).

From that day to this the further man goes in disobedience to God, the more he experiences fear. The converse is also true. The more man obeys God, learns about God and leans upon Him for every need, the less he experiences fear. The universal nature of fear is easily seen in the fact that the Lord Jesus Himself so frequently admonished

45

His disciples with such phrases as "fear not, little flock," "be not faithless, but believing," "O ye of little faith," and "Let not your heart be troubled, neither let it be afraid." Never in the history of the world has the universal problem of fear gripped so many and caused such devastation in the minds and bodies of men as the day in which we live. World conditions are not conducive to peace and faith today, for they cause many to lose their moorings and be afraid.

It is comforting for the child of God, in the face of such fear reaction to world conditions, to heed the words of the Lord Jesus Christ who said, "Ye shall hear of wars and rumors of wars: *see that ye be not troubled*" (Matthew 24:6). Even though fear is universal, God's children *do not* have to be dominated by this vicious emotional destroyer.

Fear, like anger, takes many forms. The accompanying chart describes the main variations.

The Emotional Cost of Fear

Every year countless thousands of individuals fall into mental and emotional collapse because of fear. Electric shock treatments and insulin shock treatments are becoming more and more common as forms of treatment to patients suffering from the tyrannical force of fear. Many a fearful person draws into a shell and lets life pass him by, never experiencing the rich things that God has in store for him, simply because he is afraid. The tragedy of it all is that most of the things he fears never happen.

46

EXPRESSIONS OF FEAR

ANXIETY	WORRY
DOUBTS	INFERIORITY
TIMIDITY	COWARDICE
INDECISION	SUSPICION
SUPERSTITION	HESITANCY
WITHDRAWAL	DEPRESSION
LONELINESS	HAUGHTINESS
OVERAGGRESSION	SOCIAL SHYNESS

I counseled a woman who ten years before drove her husband from her because she was so emotionally upset due to fear. She became obsessed with the idea that another woman was going to take her husband away from her, and her emotionally upset mind caused such erratic and abnormal behavior in the home that she drove her husband away from her, though the "other woman" never existed.

The emotional cost of fear is very clearly seen in this statement by Dr. S. I. McMillen. "About nine million Americans suffer from emotional and mental illness. As many hospital beds are filled by the mentally deranged as are occupied by all the medical and surgical patients combined. In fact, one out of every twenty Americans will have a psychotic disturbance severe enough to confine him in a hospital for the insane. Mental disease is indeed the nation's No. 1 health problem. What does it cost to take care of the patients in our mental hospitals? The annual cost is about one billion·dollars. Besides, outside the asylums there are a vast number who do not need confinement but who are incapable of supporting themselves. They work little or not at all and constitute a great burden on the taxpayer."[1] This cost does not include the heartache and confusion in the families from which these patients are admitted to sanitariums and asylums. Mothers or fathers are left to raise children single-handedly, and children often go untrained or uncared for as a result of emotional illness of one parent or the other.

The Social Cost of Fear
The social cost of fear is perhaps the easiest to bear, but it is expensive nonetheless. Fear-dominated individuals do not make enjoyable company. Their pessimistic and complaining spirit causes them to be shunned and avoided, thus further deepening their emotional disturbances. Many otherwise likeable and happy people are scratched off social lists and cause their companions to be equally limited simply because of ungrounded fears.

The Physical Cost of Fear
Fear, like anger, produces emotional stress, and we have already seen that medically speaking this accounts for two-thirds or more of all physical illness today.

Some of the diseases mentioned by Dr. McMillen

are high blood pressure, heart trouble, kidney disease, goiter, arthritis, headaches, strokes and most of the same 51 illnesses which he listed as caused by anger. In illustrating the effect of fear upon the human heart, he quotes Dr. Roy R. Grinker, one of the medical directors of Michael Reese Hospital in Chicago. "This doctor states that anxiety places more stress on the heart than any other stimulus, including physical exercise and fatigue."[2]

The Lord Jesus said in His Sermon on the Mount, "Take no thought for your life, what ye shall eat, or what ye shall drink; nor yet for your body, what ye shall put on...." (Matthew 6:25) Literally, that is "take no anxious thought." Again the Holy Spirit tells us, "Be anxious for nothing" (Philippians 4:6). Anxiety and worry which stem from fear cause untold physical suffering, limitations and premature death not only to non-Christians, but also to Christians who disobey the admonition to: "commit thy way unto the Lord and trust also in Him" (Psalm 37:5).

One day I called upon what I thought was an older woman who was bedridden. I was amazed to find that she was fifteen to twenty years younger than I had estimated. She made herself old before her time by being a professional worrier. As gently and yet as truthfully as I could, I tried to show her that she should learn to trust the Lord and not worry about everything. Her reaction was so typical it bears repeating. With fire in her eye and a flash of anger in her voice she asked, "Well, someone has to worry about things, don't they?" "Not if you have a heavenly Father who loves you and is interested in every detail of your life," I replied. But that dear sister didn't get the point. I hope you do!

Thank God we are not orphans! We live in a society that accepts the concept that we are the products of a biological accident and a long unguided process of evolution. That popular theory is not only incorrect but is enslaving mankind in a prison house of physical torture due to fear. If you are a Christian, memorize Philippians 4:6, 7, and every time you find yourself worrying or becoming anxious, pray. Thank God that you have a heavenly Father who is interested in your problems, and turn them over to Him. Your little shoulders are not broad enough to carry the weight of the world or even your own family problems, but the Lord Jesus "is able to do exceeding abundantly above all that we ask or think" (Ephesians 3:20).

The Spiritual Cost of Fear

The spiritual cost of fear is very similar to the spiritual cost of anger. It quenches or stifles the Holy Spirit, which keeps us from being effective in this life and steals many of our rewards in the life to come. Fear keeps us from being joyful, happy, radiant Christians and instead makes us thankless, complaining, defeated Christians who are unfaithful. A fearful person is not going to manifest the kind of life that encourages a sinner to come to him and say, "Sir, what must I do to be saved?" If Paul and Silas had let their fears predominate, the Philippian jailer would never have been converted and we would not have the great salvation verse, Acts 16:31.

Fear keeps the Christian from pleasing God. The Bible tells us, "Without faith it is impossible to please God" (Hebrews 11:6). The eleventh chapter of Hebrews, which is called the "Faith Chapter," names men whose biography is given in sufficient detail throughout the Scriptures to establish that they represent all four of the basic temperament types. The thing that made these men acceptable in the sight of God is that they were not overcome by their natural weakness of either fear or anger, but walked with God by faith. Consider these four men representative of the four temperament types: Peter the Sanguine, Paul the Choleric, Moses the Melancholy and Abraham the Phlegmatic. It is difficult to find more dynamic illustrations of the power of God working in the lives of men than these four. "God is no respecter of persons." What He did to strengthen their weaknesses He will do through His Holy Spirit for you!

What Causes Fear?

Because fear is such a universal experience of man and because most of the readers of this book will be parents who can help their children avoid this tendency, I would like to answer this question simply in layman's terms. There are at least eight causes of fear.

1. *Temperament traits.* We have already seen that the melancholy and phlegmatic temperaments are

indecisive and fear-prone. Although Mr. Sanguine is not nearly as self-confident as his blustering way would have us believe, he too can become fearful. Very few cholerics would not have some melancholy or phlegmatic tendencies, so that conceivably all people will have a temperament tendency toward fear, though some more than others.

2. *Childhood experiences.* Psychologists and psychiatrists agree that the basic needs of man are love, understanding and acceptance. The most significant human thing that parents can do for their children—short of leading one's children to a saving knowledge of Jesus Christ—is to give them the warmth and security of parental love. This does not exclude discipline or the teaching of submission to standards and principles. In fact, it is far better for a child to learn to adjust to rules and standards in the loving atmosphere of his home than in the cruel world outside. There are, however, two specific parental habits I suggest you diligently avoid:

Overprotection. An overprotective parent makes a child self-centered and fearful of the very things happening to him that his parent is afraid will happen. Children quickly learn to read our emotions. Their bodies can far more easily absorb the falls, burns and shocks of life than their emotions can absorb our becoming tense, upset or hysterical over these minor experiences. The fearful mother that forbids her son to play football probably does far more harm to his emotional development by her repeated suggestions of fear than the damage done to Junior if his front teeth were knocked out or his leg broken. Legs heal and teeth can be replaced, but it takes a miracle of God to remove the scar tissues of fear from our emotions.

Dominating children. Angry, explosive parents who dominate the lives of their children or who critically pounce upon every failure in their lives often create hesitancy, insecurity and fear in them. Children need correction, but they need it done in the proper spirit. Whenever we have to point out our children's mistakes, we should also make it a practice to note their strengths and good points, or at least criticize them in such a way as to let them know that they are still every bit as much the object of our love as they were before.

The Spirit-filled parent is inspired through his loving, compassionate nature to build others up and to show approval whenever possible. Even in the times of correction he will convey his love. To do otherwise with our children is to leave lasting fear-scars on their emotions.

3. *A traumatic experience.* Child assault or molesting leaves a lasting emotional scar that often carries over into adulthood, causing fear concerning the act of marriage. Other tragic experiences in childhood frequently set fear-patterns into motion that last throughout life.

During the past few years our family has enjoyed some wonderful occasions water skiing. The only member of the family that has not tried it is my wife, and she is deathly afraid of the water. I have begged her, encouraged her and done everything I could to entice her to get over this fear of the water, but to no avail. Finally last summer I gave up. She made one Herculean attempt to overcome this fear by donning a wetsuit that could easily sustain her body in water. She then put on a life jacket, which also by itself could sustain her in water, and very hesitantly lowered herself over the side of the boat. The moment her hand left the security of the boat and she was floating freely in the water, I noted a look of terror in her eyes. For the first time I really understood how frightened she was of the water. Upon questioning her, I found that it all went back to a childhood experience in Missouri when she came within an eyelash of drowning. These experiences leave hidden marks on a person's emotions that often follow them through life.

4. *A negative thinking pattern.* A negative thinking pattern or defeatist complex will cause a person to be fearful of attempting any new thing. The moment we start suggesting to ourselves "I can't, I can't, I can't" we are almost certain of failure. Our mental attitude makes even ordinary tasks difficult to perform when we approach them with a negative thought. Repeated failures or refusal to do what our contemporaries are able to accomplish often causes further breakdown in self-confidence and increases fear. A Christian need never be dominated by this negative habit. By memorizing Philippians 4:13 and seeking the Spirit's power in applying it, one can gain a positive attitude toward life.

5. *Anger.* Anger, as pointed out in the previous chapter, can produce fear. I have counseled with

individuals who had indulged bitterness and anger until they erupted in such explosive tirades that they afterward admitted, "I'm afraid of what I might do to my own child."

6. *Sin*. "If our heart condemn us not, then have we confidence toward God" (I John 3:21) is a principle that cannot be violated without producing fear. Every time we sin, our conscience reminds us of our relationship to God. This has often been misconstrued by psychiatrists who blame religion for creating guilt complexes in people which, they said, in turn produced fear. A few years ago our family doctor, who at that time was not a Christian, made the following statement to me: "You ministers, including my saintly old father, do irreparable damage to the emotional life of men by preaching the gospel." I questioned his reason for such a statement and he said, "I took my internship in a mental institution, and the overwhelming majority of those people had a religious background and were there because of fear induced by guilt complexes."

The next day I attended a ministers' meeting where Dr. Clyde Narramore gave a lecture on pastoral counseling. During the question period I told him of the previous day's conversation and asked his opinion. Dr. Narramore instantly replied: "That is not true. People have guilt complexes because they are guilty!" The result of sin is a consciousness of guilt, and guilt causes fear in modern man just as it did to Adam and Eve in the Garden of Eden. A simple remedy for this is: "Walk in the way of the Lord."

7. *Lack of faith.* Lack of faith, even in a Christian's life, can produce fear. I have noticed in counseling that fear caused by lack of faith is basically confined to two common areas.

The first is fear concerning the sins of the past. Because the Christian does not know what the Bible teaches in relationship to confessed sin, he has not come to really believe that God has cleansed him from all sin (I John 1:9). Sometime ago I counseled with a lady who was in such a protracted period of fear that she had sunk into deep depression. We found that one of her basic problems was that she was still haunted by a sin committed eleven years before. All during this time she had been a Christian but had gone through a complete emotional collapse, haunted by the fear of that past sin.

When I asked if she had confessed that sin in the name of Jesus Christ, she replied, "Oh, yes, many times." I then gave her a spiritual prescription to make a Bible study of all Scripture verses that deal with the forgiveness of sins. When she came back into my office two weeks later, she was not the same woman. For the first time in her life she really understood how God regarded her past sin, and when she began to agree with Him that it was "remembered against her no more," she got over that fear.

A man I counseled who had a similar problem gave me a slightly different answer when I asked, "Have you confessed that sin to Christ?" "Over a thousand times," was his interesting reply. I told him that was 999 times too many. He should have confessed it once and thanked God 999 times that

He had forgiven him for that awful sin. The Word of God is the cure for this problem, because "Faith cometh by hearing, and hearing by the Word of God" (Romans 10:17).

The second area in which men are prone to be fearful because of lack of faith concerns the future. If the devil can't get them to worry about their past sins, he will seek to get them to worry about God's provision in the future, and thus they are not able to enjoy the riches of God's blessing today. The Psalmist has said, "This is the day which the Lord hath made; we will rejoice and be glad in it" (Psalm 118:24). People who enjoy life are not "living tomorrow" nor worrying about the past; they are living today.

If you are worrying about tomorrow, you can't possibly enjoy today. The interesting thing is that you can't give God tomorrow; you can only give Him what you have, and you have today. Dr. Cramer quoted a comment by Mr. John Watson in the *Houston Times* which read:

"What does your anxiety do? It does not empty tomorrow of its sorrow, but it empties today of its strength. It does not make you escape the evil; it makes you unfit to cope with it if it comes."[3]

Now I think you are about ready to face the primary cause of fear. The above seven causes of fear are only contributing factors. The basic cause for fear is . . .

8. *Selfishness.* As much as we don't like to face this ugly word, it is a fact nonetheless. We are fearful because we are selfish. Why am I afraid? Because I

am interested in self. Why am I embarrassed when I stand before an audience? Because I don't wish to make a fool of myself. Why am I afraid I will lose my job? Because I am afraid of being a failure in the eyes of my family or not being able to provide my family and myself with the necessities of life. Excuse it if you will, but all fear can be traced basically to the sin of selfishness.

Don't Be a Turtle

A Christian woman went to a Christian psychologist and asked, "Why am I so fearful?" He asked several questions. "When you enter a room, do you feel that everyone is looking at you?" "Yes," she said. "Do you often have the feeling your slip is showing?" "Yes." When he discovered she played the piano he asked, "Do you hesitate to volunteer to play the piano at church for fear someone else can do so much better?" "How did you know?" was her reply. "Do you hesitate to entertain others in your home?" Again she said, "Yes." Then he proceeded to tell her kindly that she was a very selfish young woman. "You are like a turtle," he said. "You pull into your shell and peek out only as far as necessary. If anyone gets too close, you pop your head back inside your shell for protection. That shell is selfishness. Throw it away and start thinking more about others and less about yourself."

The young lady went back to her room in tears. She never thought of herself as selfish, and it crushed her when she was confronted with the awful truth. Fortunately, she went to God, and He has gradually cured her of that vicious sin. Today she is truly a "new creature." She entertains with abandon, has completely thrown off the old "shell," and consequently enjoys a rich and abundant life.

Walking in the Spirit

"Walking in the Spirit" and being filled by the Holy Spirit are not the same thing, though they are very closely related. "This I say then, Walk in the Spirit, and ye shall not fulfill the lust of the flesh" (Galatians 5:16). "If we live in the Spirit, let us also walk in the Spirit" (Galatians 5:25). Having followed the five simple rules for the filling of the Holy Spirit, one may walk in the Spirit by guarding against quenching or grieving the Spirit and by following the above five steps each time he is aware that sin has crept into his life. Being filled with the Holy Spirit is not a single experience that lasts for life. On the contrary, it must be repeated many times. In fact, at first it should be repeated many times daily. This can be done while kneeling at your place of devotion, at the breakfast table, in the car en route to work, while sweeping the kitchen floor, while listening to a telephone conversation—in fact, anywhere. In effect, walking in the Spirit puts one in continual communion with God, which is the same as abiding in Christ. To "walk in the Spirit" is to be freed of your weaknesses. Yes, even your greatest weaknesses can be overcome by the Holy Spirit. Instead of being dominated by your weaknesses, you can be dominated by the Holy Spirit. That is God's will for all Christians.

3-22-79

REFERENCES
1. S. I. McMillen, *None of These Diseases*, © Fleming H. Revell Company, p. 116.
2. *Ibid.*, page 62.
3. Cramer, *op. cit.*, page 28.

O O O